The
HERSHEY'S™
KISSES™
Addition Book

by Jerry Pallotta
Illustrated by Rob Bolster

Cartwheel
·B·O·O·K·S·®
SCHOLASTIC INC.

New York   Toronto   London   Auckland   Sydney   Mexico City   New Delhi   Hong Kong

Thank you to R. Michael Hechtman and Dr. Judi Hechtman.
—— *Jerry Pallotta*

This book is dedicated to all the men and women who make their living as clowns.
—— *Rob Bolster*

© 2001 Hershey Foods Corporation Trademarks used
under license, Corporate Board Books Inc., Licensee.

Text copyright © 2001 by Jerry Pallotta.
Illustrations copyright © 2001 by Rob Bolster.
All rights reserved. Published by Scholastic Inc.
SCHOLASTIC, CARTWHEEL BOOKS and associated logos
are trademarks and/or registered trademarks of Scholastic Inc.

Library of Congress Cataloging-in-Publication Data available.

ISBN 0-439-26728-5

10 9 8 7 6 5 4 3 2 1   01 02 03 04 05

Printed in Mexico   49
This edition first printing, May 2001

HERSHEY'S
OFFICIAL LICENSED PRODUCT

MILK CHOCOLATE PLUS MATH EQUALS FUN!

Here are some math terms that will help you while reading this book.

This is a plus sign. It is used for addition.

This is a minus sign. It is used for subtraction.

This is an equal sign. It is used to show that two or more numbers are equal in value.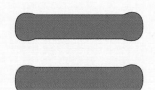

This is a piece of candy. In this book we count and add with HERSHEY'S KISSES™ chocolates.

This is a clown. There will be no clowning around in this book. This is a serious math book.

1+1=2

Let's start off with a very simple equation. One plus one equals two.
Adding two or more numbers together is called "addition."
This is an addition book.

2+1=3

When the numbers on each side of an equal sign have the same value, it is called an equation. Here is another simple equation.
Two plus one equals three.

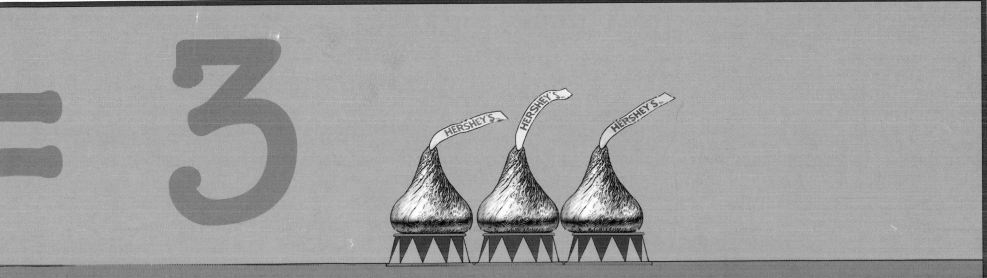

3+1=4

Three plus one equals what? The answer is four. In math, we say the "sum" is four or the "total" is four. Three plus one equals four.

4+1=5

Four plus one equals five. That is easy to see.
Look closely, though—if we keep on adding one, it is just like counting.
One, two, three, four, five, six, seven, eight, nine, ten.
Counting by one is the same as adding one at a time.

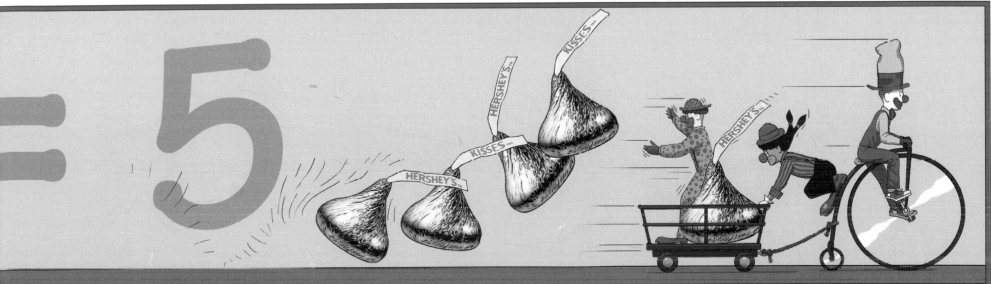

5+1=6

Five plus one equals six. Basic math is called "arithmetic." Arithmetic is addition, subtraction, multiplication, and division. Reading, writing, and arithmetic are very important.

6+1=7

Six plus one equals seven. Uh-oh! Here comes a guy with a pie. Hey, that rhymes. No pie throwing. Splat! Oh, no! You clowns, please stop goofing off while kids are learning basic addition facts.

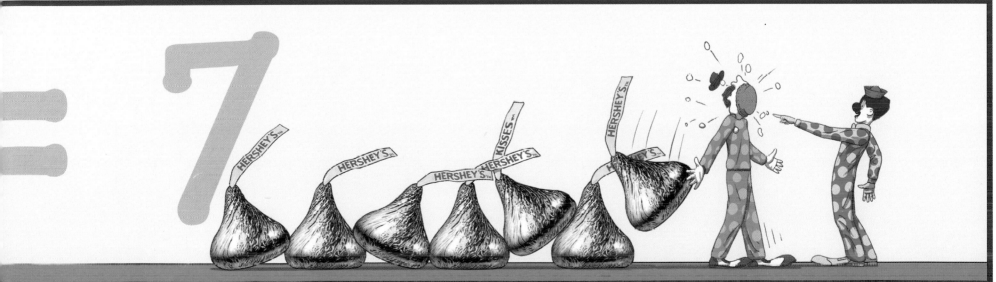

Okay, you get the idea. Here are all the equations you can
make when you add the number one to each of the numbers one through nine.
In each equation, we can switch the numbers we are adding
and still get the same answer.

1 + 1 = 2	1 + 1 = 2
2 + 1 = 3	1 + 2 = 3
3 + 1 = 4	1 + 3 = 4
4 + 1 = 5	1 + 4 = 5
5 + 1 = 6	1 + 5 = 6
6 + 1 = 7	1 + 6 = 7
7 + 1 = 8	1 + 7 = 8
8 + 1 = 9	1 + 8 = 9
9 + 1 = 10	1 + 9 = 10

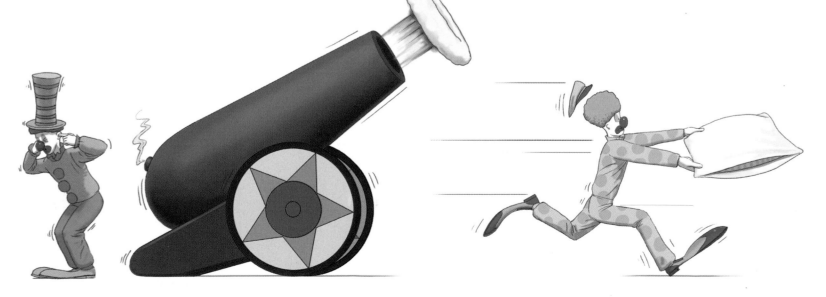

Oops! We forgot a very important equation.

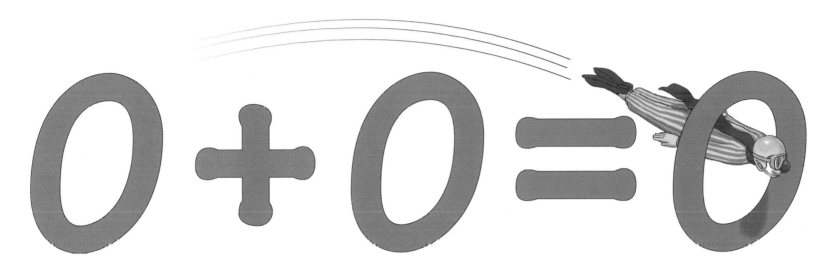

Zero plus zero equals zero.
If you have nothing and then you add nothing to
that, you still have nothing. Zero is a number, but it has no value.
Zero pieces of candy is a sad thought!

$0 + 1 = 1$

$0 + 2 = 2$

$0 + 3 = 3$

$0 + 4 = 4$

$0 + 5 = 5$

$0 + 6 = 6$

$0 + 7 = 7$

$0 + 8 = 8$

$0 + 9 = 9$

$0 + 10 = 10$

2+2=4

Toot! Toot! All aboard!
We are now doing equations that add the same number.
Two plus two equals four. When you add two numbers that are the same,
it is just like doubling the number.

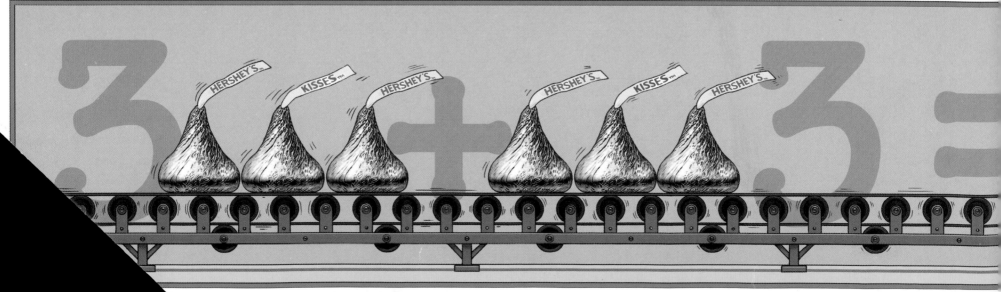

3+3=6

Three plus three equals six. If you put the answer first, it is called "reversing the equation." 6 = 3+3 Six equals three plus three.

4 + 4 = 8

Four plus four is just one of nine addition pairs that add up to eight.
Zero plus eight; one plus seven; two plus six; three plus five; four plus four;
five plus three; six plus two; seven plus one; and eight plus zero.
Do you notice a pattern?

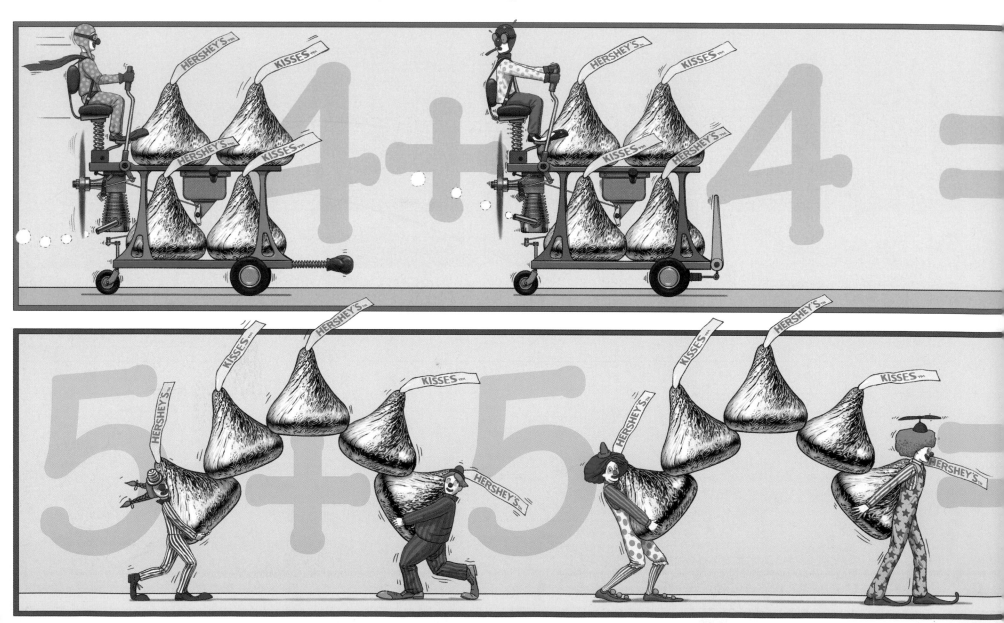

5 + 5 = 10

Five plus five equals ten. Hooray! The clowns made it to ten, a double-digit number! As you can see, the more candy we add, the more crowded the pages get. How do you like the arch?

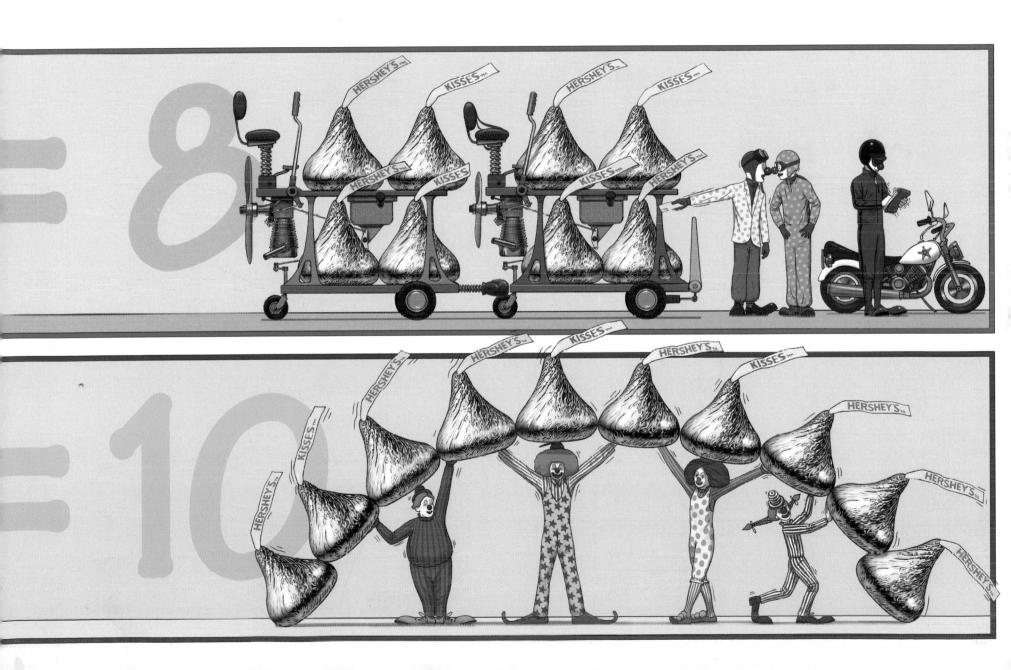

Here are some more addition facts.
Which clown's hairdo is your favorite?

0 + 2 = 2	0 + 3 = 3
1 + 2 = 3	1 + 3 = 4
2 + 2 = 4	2 + 3 = 5
3 + 2 = 5	3 + 3 = 6
4 + 2 = 6	4 + 3 = 7
5 + 2 = 7	5 + 3 = 8
6 + 2 = 8	6 + 3 = 9
7 + 2 = 9	7 + 3 = 10
8 + 2 = 10	8 + 3 = 11
9 + 2 = 11	9 + 3 = 12
10 + 2 = 12	10 + 3 = 13

Each addition fact in this book is made up of "addends" and a "sum." The addends are on one side of the equal sign and the sum is on the other.

0 + 4 = 4   5 = 5 + 0
1 + 4 = 5   6 = 5 + 1
2 + 4 = 6   7 = 5 + 2
3 + 4 = 7   8 = 5 + 3
4 + 4 = 8   9 = 5 + 4
5 + 4 = 9   10 = 5 + 5
6 + 4 = 10   11 = 5 + 6
7 + 4 = 11   12 = 5 + 7
8 + 4 = 12   13 = 5 + 8
9 + 4 = 13   14 = 5 + 9
10 + 4 = 14   15 = 5 + 10

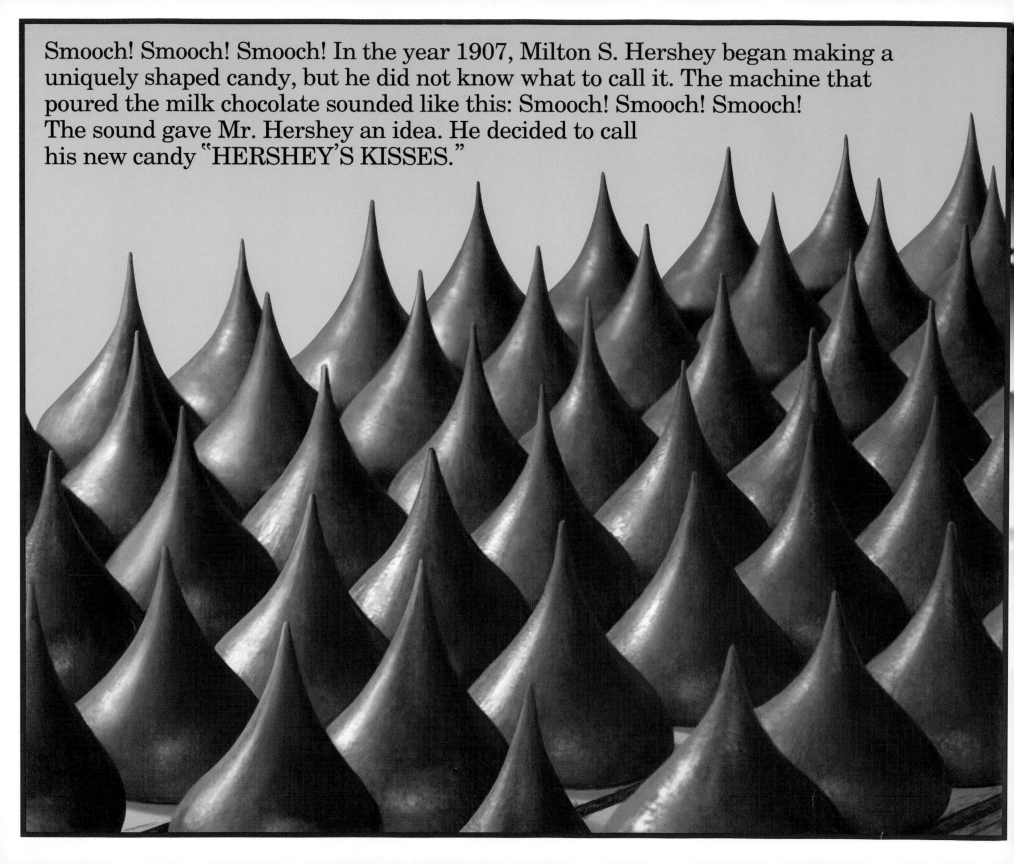

Smooch! Smooch! Smooch! In the year 1907, Milton S. Hershey began making a uniquely shaped candy, but he did not know what to call it. The machine that poured the milk chocolate sounded like this: Smooch! Smooch! Smooch! The sound gave Mr. Hershey an idea. He decided to call his new candy "HERSHEY'S KISSES."

Of course, equations can be done vertically too. Six plus six equals twelve. Whoa! We have a mistake! There is no need for an equal sign next to the sum when adding numbers vertically. What is above the line and below the line is equal.

$$\begin{array}{r} 7 \\ + \ 7 \\ \hline 14 \end{array}$$

That's better!
We have removed the equal sign.
A group of seven plus a group
of seven equals fourteen.
Grouping can help you
organize, count, and add.

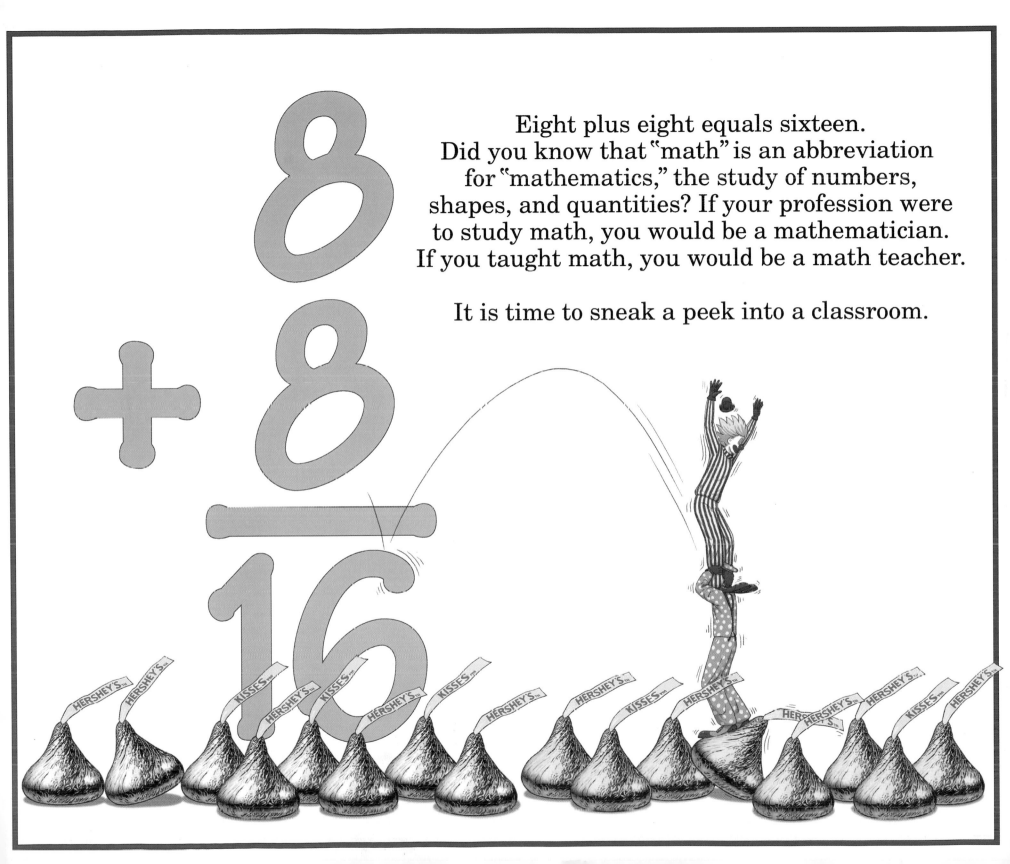

Eight plus eight equals sixteen.
Did you know that "math" is an abbreviation
for "mathematics," the study of numbers,
shapes, and quantities? If your profession were
to study math, you would be a mathematician.
If you taught math, you would be a math teacher.

It is time to sneak a peek into a classroom.

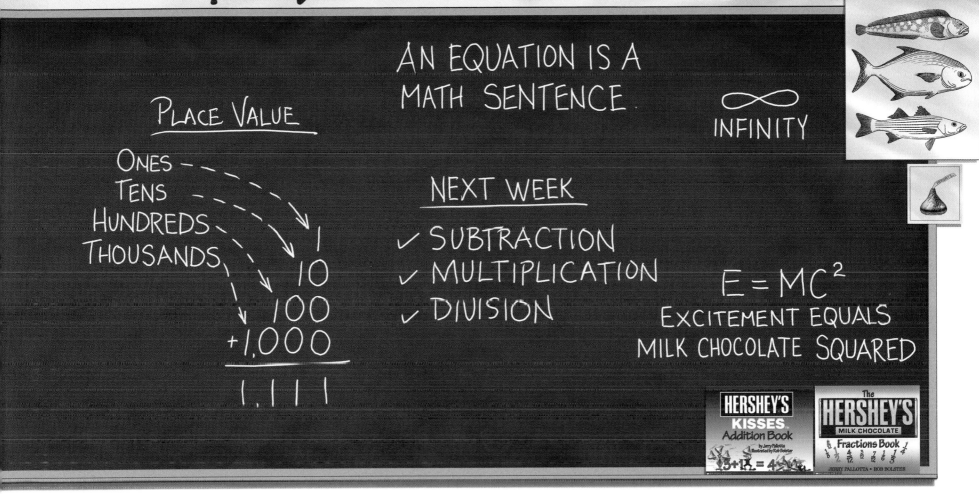

AN EQUATION IS A
MATH SENTENCE.

INFINITY

PLACE VALUE

ONES
TENS
HUNDREDS
THOUSANDS

1
10
100
+1,000
‾‾‾‾‾‾‾
1,111

NEXT WEEK

✓ SUBTRACTION
✓ MULTIPLICATION
✓ DIVISION

$E = MC^2$
EXCITEMENT EQUALS
MILK CHOCOLATE SQUARED

HERSHEY'S
KISSES
Addition Book
by Jerry Pallotta
Illustrated by Rob Bolster
3 + 1 = 4

The
HERSHEY'S
MILK CHOCOLATE
Fractions Book
JERRY PALLOTTA • ROB BOLSTER

Shhh! There is a class in progress. It's math time.
The teacher is showing the students that you can add as many
numbers as you like. There can be big numbers, small numbers,
hard equations, easy equations, lots of numbers or just a few.

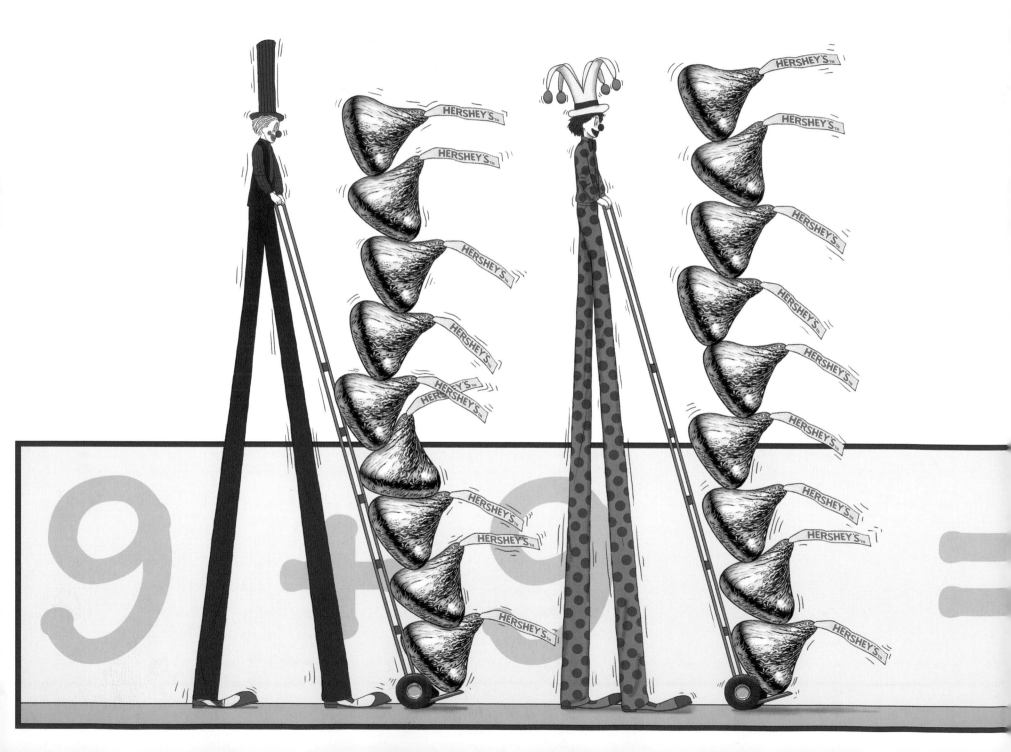

While you are adding nine plus nine, remember this . . .
there is no such thing as the biggest number in the world.
If you add one more number to it, the number becomes larger.

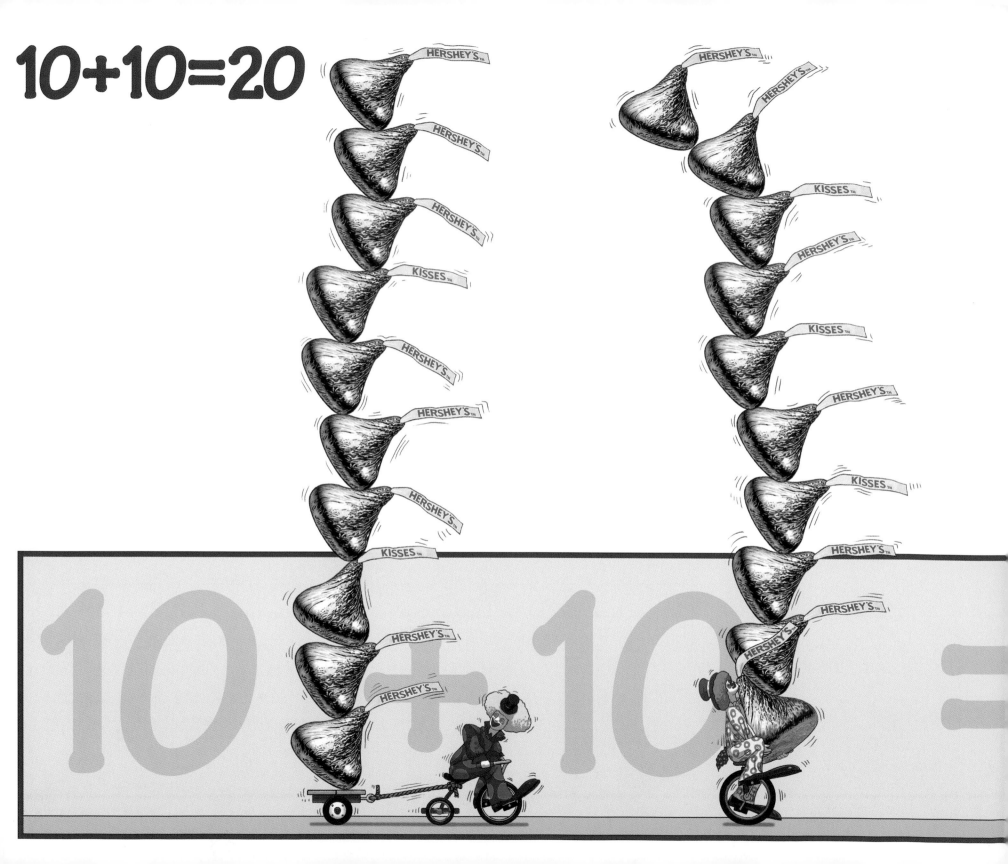

Ten plus ten equals twenty. This is our first equation that adds double-digit numbers. Here is a challenge! Make simple equations by adding only two numbers at a time. How many combinations can you make using the numbers zero through nine?

The answer is hidden on this page.

1+1+1=3

Here is a change of pace. Let's add three numbers! One plus one plus one equals three. A math teacher might say we added three "integers" or three "single-digits" or three "addends."

1+2+3=6

One plus two plus three equals six. How can you add these numbers?
We already learned that one plus two equals three. We also learned that
three plus three equals six. You do not have to add all the numbers at once.
Two at a time is fine.

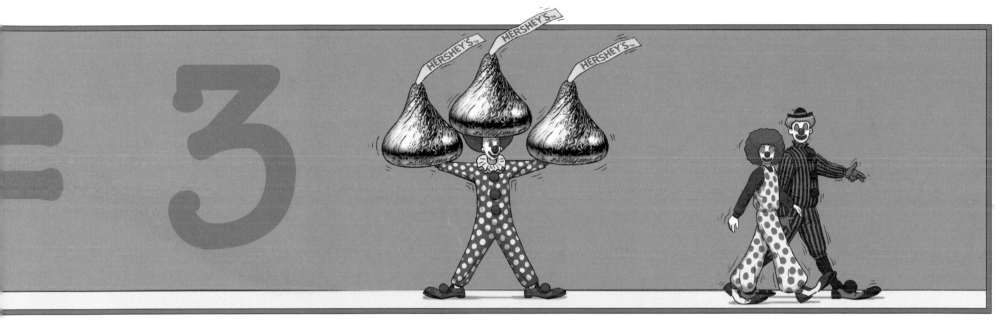

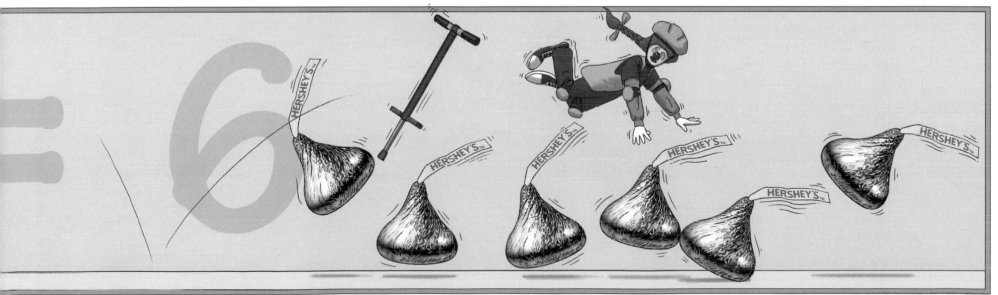

30,000,000

Are you afraid of big numbers? How about this number? Thirty million!
The Hershey's chocolate factory makes about thirty million
HERSHEY'S KISSES™ chocolates every day.

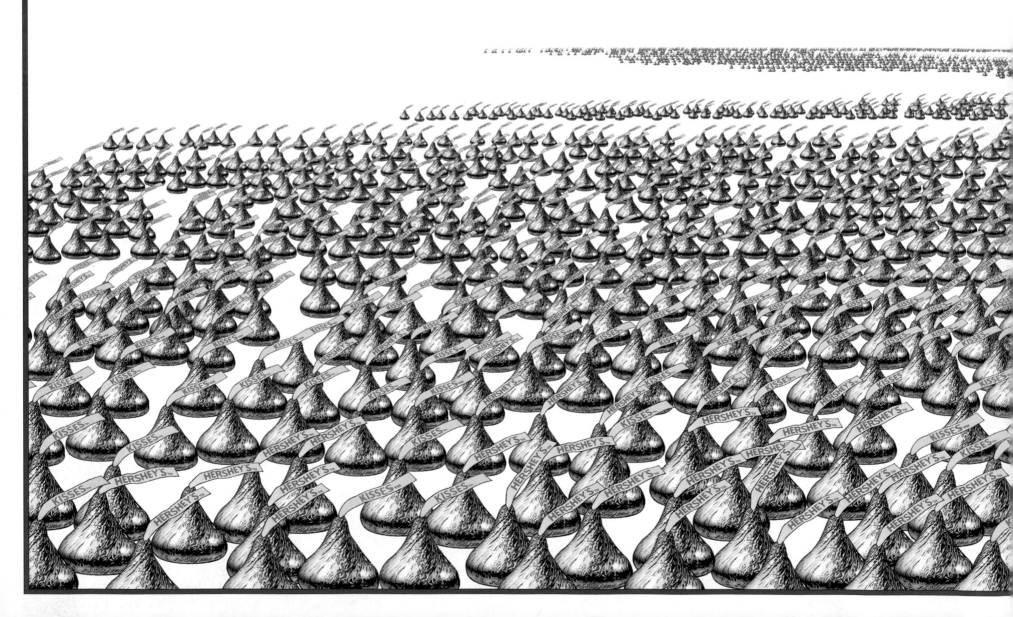

thirty million

Thirty million plus one equals thirty million and one.
Each piece of candy is wrapped in foil and topped with
a HERSHEY'S KISSES flag. Delicious!

We end this addition book with this equation:
Three minus one equals two. If you have three pieces of candy and somebody eats one of them, you will have two pieces left over. Hey, that's subtraction!

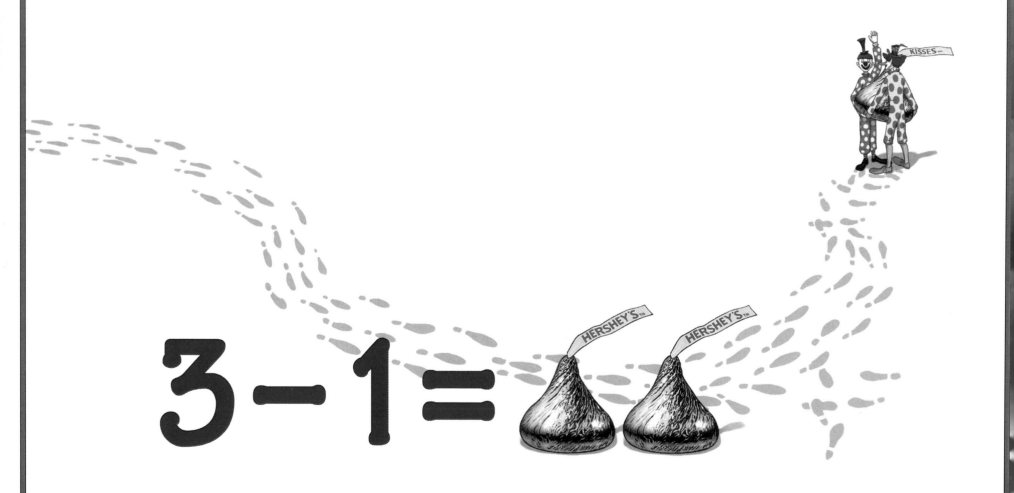